D1174069

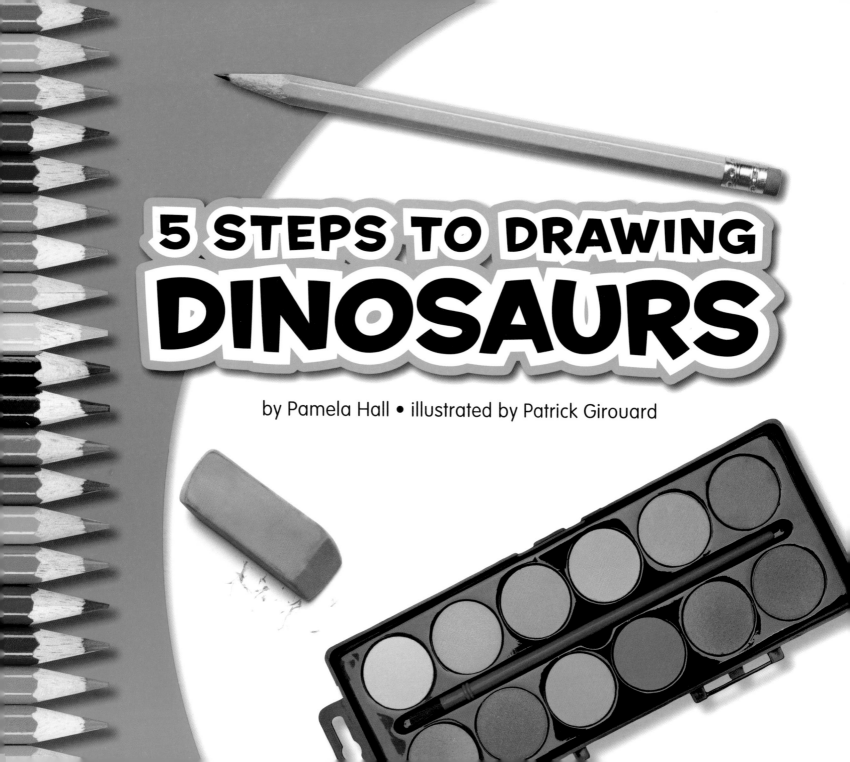

5 STEPS TO DRAWING
DINOSAURS

by Pamela Hall • illustrated by Patrick Girouard

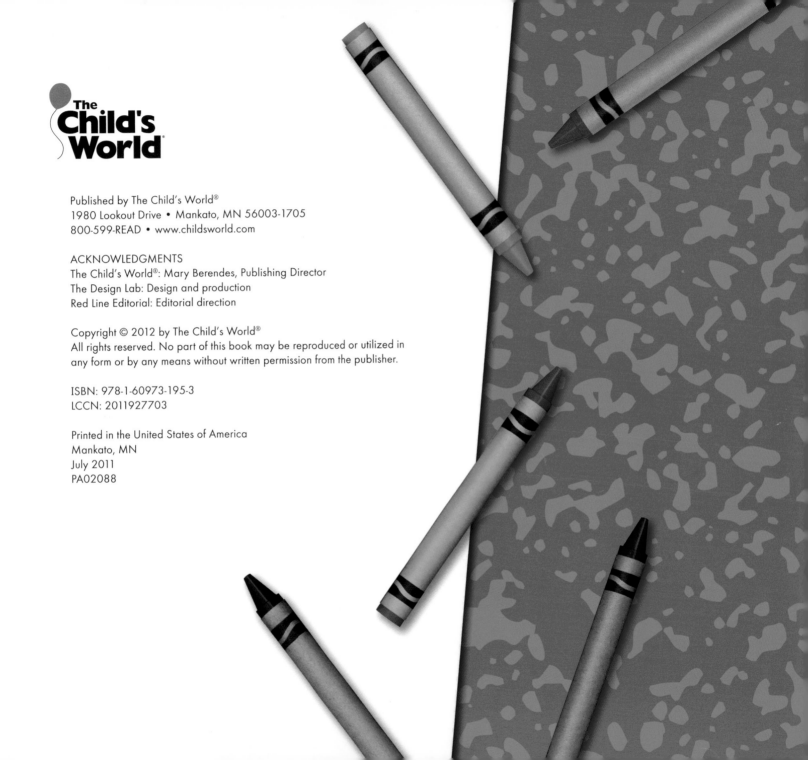

Published by The Child's World®
1980 Lookout Drive • Mankato, MN 56003-1705
800-599-READ • www.childsworld.com

ACKNOWLEDGMENTS
The Child's World®: Mary Berendes, Publishing Director
The Design Lab: Design and production
Red Line Editorial: Editorial direction

ISBN: 978-1-60973-195-3
LCCN: 2011927703

Printed in the United States of America
Mankato, MN
July 2011
PA02088

TABLE OF CONTENTS

INTRODUCTION TO DINOSAURS

Stomp, crash, roar! Dinosaurs ruled the earth for 150 million years. They were amazing creatures. But they all became **extinct** 65 million years ago. No human has ever seen one alive. How do we know they existed?

From dinosaur **fossils**! Teeth, bone, skin, and even feather fossils help us learn more about dinosaurs.

Scientists study these fossils. These clues help them learn how these creatures lived. Fossils show what they looked like, too. The word *dinosaur* means "terrible lizard." But scientists learned dinosaurs are very different from lizards. Scientists believe dinosaurs were more closely related to birds. *Tyrannosaurus rex* was very similar to a chicken. But it was a lot bigger!

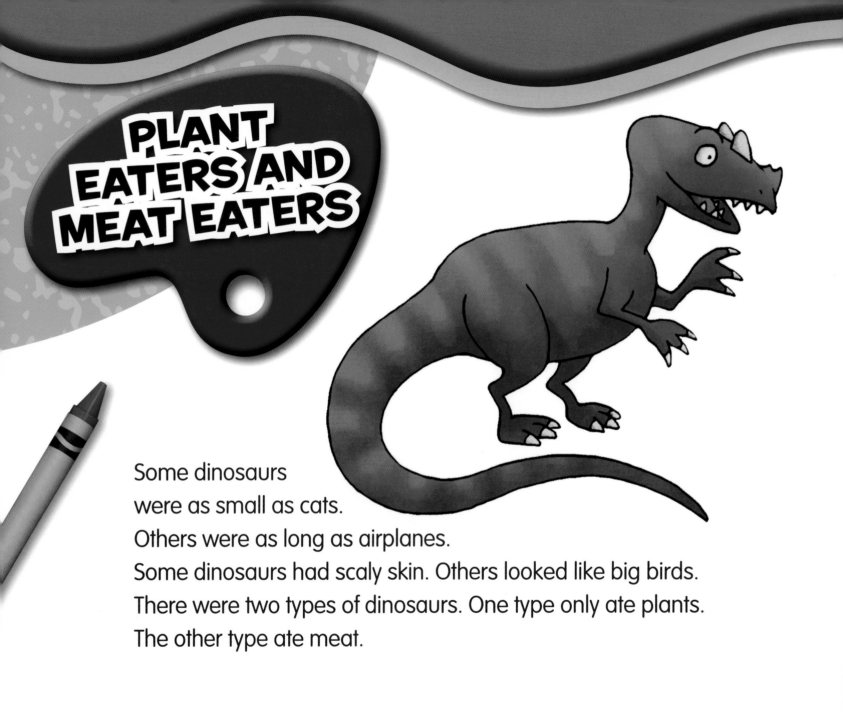

PLANT EATERS AND MEAT EATERS

Some dinosaurs
were as small as cats.

Others were as long as airplanes.

Some dinosaurs had scaly skin. Others looked like big birds.

There were two types of dinosaurs. One type only ate plants.

The other type ate meat.

Plant eaters were the longest, tallest, and heaviest of all dinosaurs. Most plant eaters walked on four legs. They ate plants all day like cows. They often became lunch for meat eaters.

Meat eaters were as tall as houses. They could walk on two legs. They could travel far and move very quickly. Meat eaters had larger brains than plant eaters. Scientists think they could plan their attacks. Meat eaters had sharp claws and teeth for fighting and tearing apart their victims.

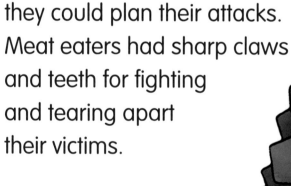

DINOSAUR PERIODS

Dinosaurs **evolved** over millions of years. Not all dinosaurs lived at the same time. They lived in different periods.

The Triassic Period was when dinosaurs started to exist. Next was the Jurassic Period. Small, winged dinosaurs started to fly. Others were able to swim in the sea. Huge plant eaters roamed on land.

The Cretaceous Period was next. Sea creatures grew larger. Huge, winged dinosaurs crossed the sky. At the end of this period, dinosaurs disappeared. Many scientists believe it was because Earth's temperature changed. A meteorite may have hit Earth, too. Then a lot of dust went into the sky and blocked the sun. Plants started to die. Soon, dinosaurs did not have enough food. They died out.

DRAWING TIPS

You've learned about dinosaurs. You're almost ready to draw them. But first, here are a few drawing tips:

Every artist needs tools. To learn how to draw dinosaurs, you will need:

- Some paper
- A pencil
- An eraser
- Markers, crayons, colored pencils, or watercolors (optional)

Anyone can learn to draw. You might think only some people can draw. That's not true. Everyone can learn to draw. It takes practice, though. The more you draw, the better you will be. With practice, you will become a true artist!

Everyone makes mistakes. This is okay! Mistakes help you learn. They help you know what not to do next time. Mistakes can even make your drawing more special. It's all right if you draw a dinosaur's legs too short. Now you've got a one-of-a-kind drawing. You can erase a mistake you don't like, too. Then start again!

Stay loose. Relax your body before you begin. Hold your pencil lightly. Don't rest your wrist on the table. Instead, move your whole arm as you draw. This will help you make smooth lines. Press lightly on the paper when you draw or erase.

Drawing is fun! The most important thing about drawing is to have fun. Be creative. Your drawings don't have to look exactly like the pictures in this book. Try changing the scales to feathers. You can also use markers, crayons, colored pencils, or watercolors to bring your dinosaurs to life.

TYRANNOSAURUS REX

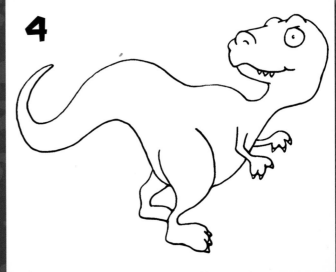

Tyrannosaurus rex had giant teeth. They were like knives. It weighed up to 14,000 pounds (6,350 kg). It stood 20 feet (6 m) high. *Tyrannosaurus rex* was the largest **predator** on Earth that could not swim or fly.

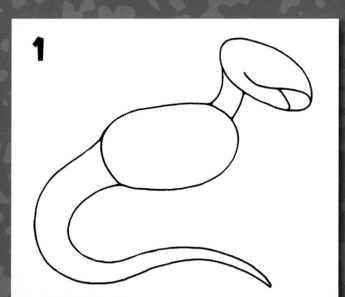

1

2

ALLOSAURUS

3

4

Allosaurus stood about 15 to 30 feet (5–9 m) tall. It was a great predator. Its huge head was filled with sharp, jagged teeth. These teeth grew, shed, and grew again.

5

1

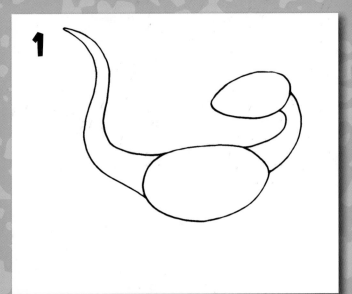

2

VELOCIRAPTOR

3

4

Velociraptor was smart and fast. It traveled in a pack. Its great eyesight let it track other dinosaurs. It used its sharp teeth and claws to rip apart food.

5

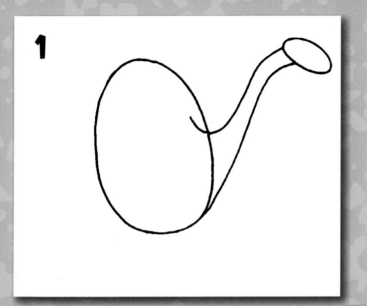

1

2

APATOSAURUS

3

4

Apatosaurus was a plant eater. It was one of the largest land creatures to roam Earth. It might have used its strong tail to fight attackers.

5

1

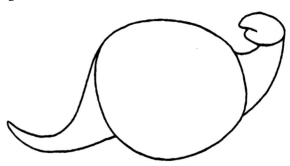

2

STEGOSAURUS

3

4

Stegosaurus was a slow-moving plant eater. Its brain was the size of a walnut. *Stegosaurus* stabbed enemies with the spikes on its tail.

1

2

TRICERATOPS

3

4

Triceratops was a plant eater. It was one of the last dinosaurs to become extinct. Its name means "three-horned face." *Triceratops* needed its horns to scare off *Tyrannosaurus rex*.

5

1

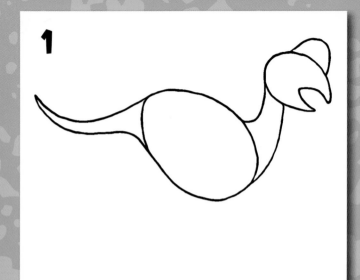

2

OVIRAPTOR

3

4

Oviraptor means "egg thief." This bird-like dinosaur couldn't fly. But it could run nearly 40 miles per hour (64 km/h). *Oviraptor* had a mean streak. It used its sharp beak to peck at small creatures.

5

1

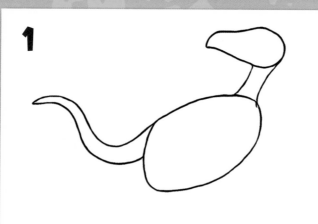

2

DROMAEOSAURUS

3

4

Dromaeosaurus had a lot in common with *Tyrannosaurus rex*. But *Dromaeosaurus* was much smaller. It was about the size of a dog. Scientists think it was covered with feathers.

MORE DRAWING

Now you know how to draw dinosaurs. Here are some ways to keep drawing them.

Dinosaurs came in all different colors, shapes, sizes, and textures. You can draw them all! Try using pens or colored pencils to draw and color in details. Experiment with crayons and markers to give your drawings different colors and textures. You can also paint your drawings. Watercolors are easy to use. If you make a mistake, you can wipe it away with a damp cloth. Try tracing the outline of your drawing with a crayon or a marker. Then paint over it with watercolor. What happens?

Drawing from Fossils

When you want something new to draw, take a field trip. Visit a museum that has dinosaur fossils. Try drawing them. First, look at the fossil carefully. Does it stand on two or four legs? How long is its tail? Now try drawing it! Use your imagination to draw its skin. Will it have feathers or scales? If you need help, use the examples in this book to guide you.

GLOSSARY

evolved (ih-VOLVD): If something evolved, it slowly changed over millions of years. Dinosaurs evolved over several time periods.

extinct (ek-STINGKT): If something is extinct, it no longer exists. Dinosaurs are extinct.

fossils (FOSS-ulz): Fossils are the remains of plants or animals that lived long ago and are found in rock. Dinosaur fossils help scientists learn about dinosaurs.

predator (PRED-uh-tur): A predator is an animal that lives by killing and eating other animals. *Tyrannosaurus rex* was a large predator.

FIND OUT MORE

BOOKS

Emberley, Ed. *Ed Emberley's Drawing Book: Make a World*. New York: Little Brown, 2006.

Long, John. *Dinosaurs*. New York: Simon & Schuster, 2007.

Winterberg, Jenna. *Dinosaurs: A Step-by-Step Drawing & Story Book*. Minneapolis, MN: Walter Foster, 2006.

WEB SITES

Visit our Web site for links about drawing dinosaurs:

childsworld.com/links

Note to Parents, Teachers, and Librarians: We routinely verify our Web links to make sure they are safe and active sites. So encourage your readers to check them out!

INDEX

ABOUT THE AUTHOR:
Pamela Hall lives near the St. Croix River in Lakeland, Minnesota, with her children and dog. Along with writing for children, Pamela enjoys being outdoors and feeding wildlife.

ABOUT THE ILLUSTRATOR:
Patrick Girouard lives and works in Indiana with his sweetheart, Debra, and their dog, Max. Patrick made his drawings on paper with ink and then painted them digitally.